I want to be a
PILOT

By Donna Baker

Illustrated by Richard Wahl

CHILDRENS PRESS, CHICAGO

Library of Congress Cataloging in Publication Data

Baker, Donna.
   I want to be a pilot.

   SUMMARY: Captain Richards describes his job as an airline pilot.
   1. Aeronautics—Juvenile literature. [1. Air pilots. 2. Occupations] I. Wahl, Richard, 1939- II. Title.
   TL547.B33   629.13'023   78-5384
   ISBN 0-516-01720-9

Copyright © 1978 by Regensteiner Publishing Enterprises, Inc.
All rights reserved. Published simultaneously in Canada.
Printed in the United States of America.
1 2 3 4 5 6 7 8 9 10 11 12 R 85 84 83 82 81 80 79 78

"Mom," Jimmy said. "I just saw our new neighbor. Did you know he was a pilot?"

"Yes, I did," said Mrs. King.

"Why is he coming home now? Dad just left for work."

"Well," said Mrs. King, "airplanes fly day and night. At some airports planes take off or land every three minutes."

Later Jimmy saw Captain Richards.

"Hi," called Jimmy.

"Hi," answered Captain Richards.

"Do you like flying?" Jimmy asked.

"Yes, I do," Captain Richards said. "Are you interested in planes?"

"Sure am," Jimmy said. "Would you like to see one? I'm taking Tammy on Saturday."

"Yes. I'll ask Mom," Jimmy said, "but I am sure I can go."

On Saturday, Jimmy, Tammy, and Captain Richards went to the airport. They passed the airport guards. Then they walked to the busy pilots' room.

"This is where I start work," Captain Richards said. "I plan my flight. Then I meet my crew."

"This is Joe Evans. He is a flight attendant. He helped my passengers on my last flight."

"These are our weather maps. Weather is very important. If I can, I plan to fly around or *over* bad weather."

Tammy walked to a big table. "What are these, Dad?"

"These are the different planes I fly. I had to learn how to fly each kind."

Jimmy looked around. "Is it hard to become a pilot?"

"It takes years, Jimmy. I took my first lessons in high school. I was in college when I got my private license. But I flew more than 350 hours before I could fly passengers.

"Even then I was not a captain. I started to work as a second officer. Then I was a co-pilot. I flew thousands of hours before I became a captain.

"Let's go to the airplane," Captain Richards said.

"Before every flight my co-pilot and I check out the plane. I look at everything and make sure it is all right. This is called a 'walk-around.' Then I check out the inside.

"This is the cockpit."

"Wow," said Jimmy. "Look at it!"

"There are a lot of instruments. They are all important. Before every flight I must test each one. If it works, I mark it off on my

check list. If something is wrong it must be fixed or I won't take off. We make sure the plane is safe."

"May I listen to the radio, Dad?"

"Sure."

"This is Ozark 539, 119 at 16,000 feet ..... right 160, Ozark 183 ..... United 628 go to 2,000 feet ..... Mid-America 357 cleared for take off ..."

Tammy laughed. "What are they saying?"

"The tower is telling the pilots where to go," Captain Richards said. "Each plane has its own place in the air and on the ground. The tower must know where each one is at all times.

"Look at that plane. Do you see those people? They are the ground crew. Some of them check the engines and landing gear. Others fuel the plane. Still others are loading the bags and the food. Everyone works to see that planes are safe and comfortable."

"By the way, is anyone hungry?" Captain Richards asked.

"Yes."

"Okay, next stop lunch."

"Captain Richards," Jimmy said, "do all pilots work for the airlines?"

"No, Jimmy, there are many kinds of pilots. Some work for business. Some

work for farmers. Others work for the government."

"I like your job," Tammy said.

"Me, too. Someday I want to be a pilot," Jimmy said.

"Great! Someday you both may fly the Space Shuttle into outer space," Captain Richards said.

SOME WORDS YOU SHOULD KNOW

airlines	flight	officer
airplane	flight attendant	outer space
airport	fuel	passengers
business	gear	pilot
captain	government	private license
check list	ground crew	second officer
cockpit	guards	Space Shuttle
comfortable	instruments	take off
co-pilot	land	tower
crew	landing gear	weather
engines	neighbor	walk-around

ABOUT THE AUTHOR:

Donna Baker lives with her husband, son, and two daughters in Arlington Heights, Illinois. The love of sharing literature of childhood with her own children encouraged her to write. Mrs. Baker has a degree in fine arts and elementary education with certification as a school librarian. She has had experience teaching second and third grades and also adults.

ABOUT THE ARTIST:

Richard Wahl, graduate of the Art Center College of Design in Los Angeles, has illustrated a number of magazine articles and booklets. He is a skilled artist and photographer who advocates realistic interpretations of his subjects. He lives with his wife and two sons in Libertyville, Illinois.